GREAT GRIZZLY BEARS

THERESA EMMINIZER

PowerKiDS
press™

New York

Published in 2022 by The Rosen Publishing Group, Inc.
29 East 21st Street, New York, NY 10010

First Edition

Portions of this work were originally authored by Therese Shea and published as *Grizzly Bears*. All new material in this edition authored by Theresa Emminizer.

Editor: Jill Keppeler
Book Design: Michael Flynn

Photo Credits: Cover, p. 1 Laura Hedien/Moment/Getty Images; (series background) Stefan Sorean/Shutterstock.com; p. 5 Ron Sanford/Corbis Documentary/Getty Images; pp. 7, 9 LuCaAr/iStock/Getty Images; p. 11 Paul Souders/Stone/Getty Images; p. 13 Richard Seeley/Shutterstock.com; p. 15 Iain Tall/iStock/Getty Images; p. 17 Tom Tietz/Shutterstock.com; p. 19 Elizabeth M. Ruggiero/iStock/Getty Images; p. 21 Daria Rybakova/Shutterstock.com.

Library of Congress Cataloging-in-Publication Data

Names: Emminizer, Theresa, author.
Title: Great grizzly bears / Theresa Emminizer.
Description: New York : PowerKids Press, [2022] | Series: Animals of the
    tundra | Includes index.
Identifiers: LCCN 2020021711 | ISBN 9781725326316 (library binding) | ISBN
    9781725326293 (paperback) | ISBN 9781725326309 (6 pack)
Subjects: LCSH: Grizzly bear–Juvenile literature. | Tundra
    animals–Juvenile literature.
Classification: LCC QL737.C27 E528 2022 | DDC 599.784–dc23
LC record available at https://lccn.loc.gov/2020021711

Manufactured in the United States of America

Some of the images in this book illustrate individuals who are models. The depictions do not imply actual situations or events.

CPSIA Compliance Information: Batch #CSPK22. For Further Information contact Rosen Publishing, New York, New York at 1-800-237-9932.

Find us on

CONTENTS

Big Bears

Grizzly bears are big! They weigh up to 800 pounds (362.9 kg) and stand up to 8 feet (2.4 m) tall! Grizzly bears need a lot of space to live. A grizzly's **range** can cover 600 square miles (1,554 sq km).

At Home in the Tundra

Grizzly bears live in the tundra of Alaska and Canada. That's an area where few trees grow. It's very cold and the ground is always frozen. Grizzly bears have **adapted** to live in this **environment**.

Keeping Out the Cold

How do grizzly bears stay warm in the tundra? Grizzlies have thick fur. They have **layers** of fat, which help hold heat inside their body. During the summer, grizzlies eat as much food as they can to build up fat.

Warm in the Winter

During winter, a grizzly digs a den. It curls up inside the den and falls into a deep sleep. Grizzly bears don't eat during winter. They live off their fat. Grizzlies can stay in their den for seven months!

Bear Families

Mother grizzlies give birth to cubs inside their den. They usually have two to four cubs at a time. Cubs stay inside the den until the snow melts. Grizzly mothers care for their cubs for about two years.

Bear Behavior

Adult grizzlies spend most of their time alone. They mark their **territory** to tell other bears to stay away. However, during summer in Alaska, many grizzly bears gather at rivers to catch salmon.

Bears are top **predators** in the tundra. They hunt fish, deer, caribou, and other animals. They also eat plants, including berries, roots, and grasses. They use their claws to dig through the dirt and find bugs to eat.

Special Skills

A grizzly's powerful shoulders make it a strong digger. Grizzlies are also good swimmers. Cubs are good climbers. Although they're large, grizzlies are also very fast. In short bursts, adults can run at speeds up to 35 miles (56.3 km) per hour.

Bears Bounce Back

Once, there were thousands of grizzly bears. As people built towns and cities, the bears' **habitat** shrank. Hunters killed so many bears that grizzlies almost died out completely. Today, there are laws to keep grizzly bears safe.

Fancy Features

Height

8 feet (2.4 m)

Weight

800 pounds
(362.9 kg)

Top speed

35 miles
(56.3 km)
per hour

GLOSSARY

adapt: To change in order to live better in a certain environment.

environment: The conditions that surround a living thing and affect the way it lives.

habitat: The natural home for plants, animals, and other living things.

layer: One part of something lying over or under another.

predator: An animal that eats another animal.

range: An open area of land over which animals move and feed.

territory: An area that an animal or a group of animals uses and defends.

FOR MORE INFORMATION

WEBSITES

Grizzly Bear
www.nwf.org/Educational-Resources/Wildlife-Guide/Mammals/Grizzly-Bear
The National Wildlife Federation presents this site full of facts about grizzlies, including range, behavior, description, and conservation.

Grizzly Bear
www.nationalgeographic.com/animals/mammals/g/grizzly-bear/
Get a look at photos of grizzly bears and learn more about this huge animal on this National Geographic website.

BOOKS

Carney, Elizabeth. *Bears.* Washington, D.C.: National Geographic, 2016.

Poole, H. W. *Grizzly Bears.* New York, NY: Children's Press, Scholastic Inc., 2019.

INDEX